ISBN : 979-8-89122-246-5

# Dedication

**This book is dedicated to David for always encouraging my creativity and to Donna for challenging me to follow through with my wild ideas.**

# About the Author

**Beth Grace is an educator who is passionate about creating enjoyable academic atmospheres and teaching people about learning differences and how those differences don't have to be disabilities.**

The first day of school was always filled with hope. A new box of crayons, a fresh notebook, and even a pair of new shoes.

"I'm going to put a rock on your head if you don't stop growing!" my dad would joke.

HARDWARE store

It was fun, and I loved learning. Reading, math, science, history it all came easily to me.

However, as I grew older, arithmetic became increasingly difficult. I had memorized most multiplication tables, but in my desperation to do well, I cheated on a test. The guilt was overwhelming, so I confessed to my teacher.

Test
Today

**Math class became a source of dread, with its complex word problems and numerous steps.**

**Fact families and fractions, I found them frightful.**

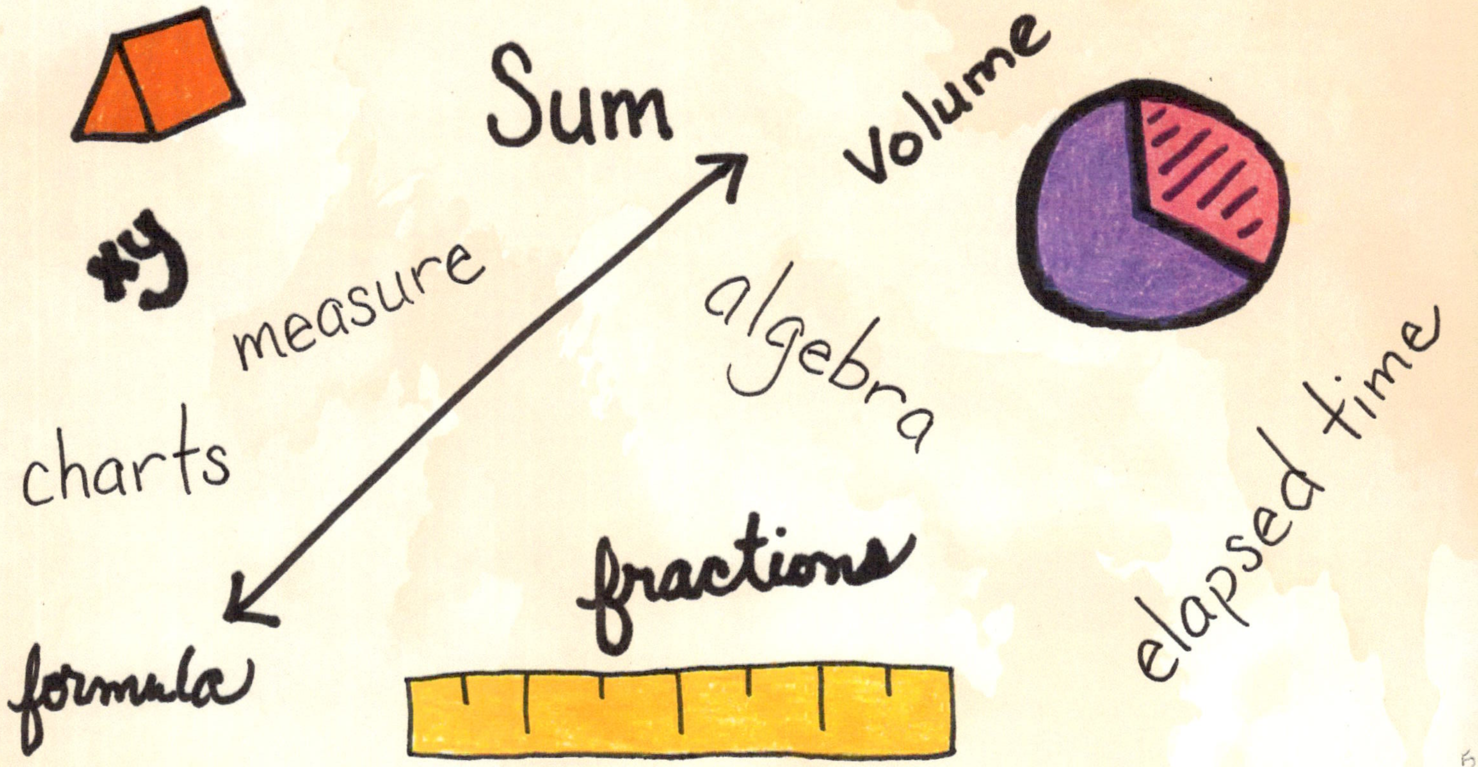

How was it possible that someone who excelled in reading, played musical instruments, wrote poems and stories, drew pictures, and had an amazing imagination struggled to solve math problems? Everyone else in the class could do it.

combine
64 ÷ 8
product
equal parts
3/5 =
9 x 2
75
- .50
difference
total
?

**Each school year brought new challenges, and despite my mom's help, I couldn't recall the solutions by the next day.**

My imagination turned against me, filling me with fears of failure and embarrassment. I felt dumb.

Algebra, geometry, or even basic money math – none made sense to me. At my father's store, the thought of making change for customers made me nauseous.

One teacher even told me, "You need to learn to make biscuits and catch a rich man to marry." I kept working but passed each class barely.

I continued to prioritize my weaknesses over my strengths until I met Mrs. Martin.

Rather than worksheets on number lines, she had us create lifesized number lines. We baked in class, learned measurements, and then enjoyed the brownies we had made.

Would you rather have 1/3 or 1/2 of the brownies?

Each class with Mrs. Martin was a delight, and I started looking forward to it.

We played games and practiced math facts. Before I knew it, Mrs. Martin had outwitted me – she made me understand.

"Mrs. Martin! I'm mad at you. You made me learn," I exclaimed.

Math MAGIC
MATH MATTERS
Keep Asking Questions.
103 - 30 = 73
Kilograms in 160.9
61 + 12 = 73
3×4=12
4×3=12
12÷3=4
12÷4=3
prime number

With a wide smile, she replied, “I led you to knowledge in the way you needed to learn it. You embraced the journey. Along the way, you added confidence.”

“But what about next year? What if my new teacher doesn’t teach like you do?”

Mrs. Martin shared a secret with me, “You have the tools you need to learn even more. Always ask questions. Teachers are there to help.”

She was right. I took what I had learned from her and built upon it. I met more wonderful teachers and even helped other students who struggled. I learned that I could rely on Mrs. Martin and many others. I also made sure they knew, “You can always count on me.”

I can't say math got easier but trying did. Making mistakes and learning from them helped me, and helping other students with what we now know is dyscalculia. That is difficulty understanding math concepts and a disruption in abilities to recall mathematical information. Now there are assessments that weren't available when I was a child.

These tests make sure students with dyscalculia get the help they need. A lot of my learning came from trial and error, but in the long run, it made me work harder. I even became a teacher because I wanted to make a difference in education and make sure that people with dyscalculia realize that "You can count on me!"

Never give up. Keep asking questions. Get help when you need it, and offer help when you can.

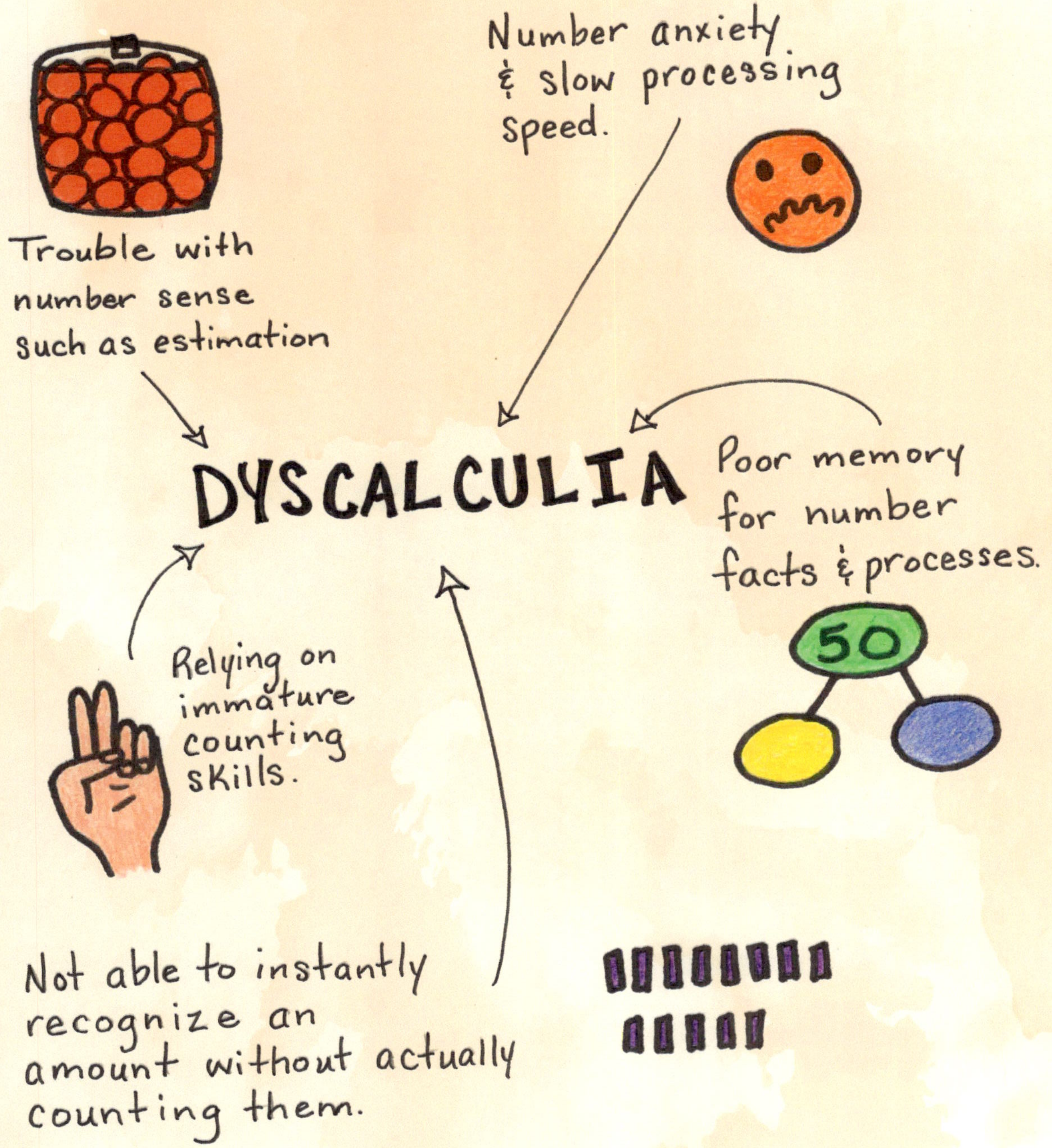
Number anxiety & slow processing speed.
Trouble with number sense such as estimation
DYSCALCULIA
Poor memory for number facts & processes.
50
Relying on immature counting skills.
Not able to instantly recognize an amount without actually counting them.

# Activities

# 1. Visual Learning with Manipulatives:

***Materials Needed:*** **Counting blocks, coins, or counters.**

## Steps:

i. Choose a simple math problem, like 4 + 3.

ii. Give the child 4 blocks to represent the first number and 3 blocks for the second number.

iii. Ask the child to count all the blocks together to find the total.

iv. Discuss the result together to reinforce the concept that 4 blocks plus 3 blocks equal 7 blocks.

## 2. Board Games Involving Numbers:

***Materials Needed:*** **Board games such as "Chutes and Ladders" or "Monopoly Junior."**

### Steps:

i. **Set up the game according to the instructions.**

ii. **Encourage the child to roll the dice and count the spaces moved aloud each turn.**

iii. **Use the game's currency for transactions, assisting in counting money and making changes.**

## 3. Cooking and Baking

***Materials Needed:*** **Recipe ingredients, measuring cups, and spoons.**

## Steps:

i. Choose a simple recipe together.
ii. Ask the child to measure specific ingredients using the appropriate measuring cups or spoons.
iii. Follow the recipe step by step, discussing each measurement and its role in the recipe.

## 4. Pattern Recognition with Colors and Shapes:

***Materials Needed:*** **Colored blocks or shapes.**

### Steps:

i. **Start by creating a simple color or shape pattern.**
ii. **Show the pattern to the child and ask them to continue it.**
iii. **Gradually increase the complexity of the patterns as the child becomes more comfortable.**

# Complete The Picture

# Complete The Picture

# Complete The Picture

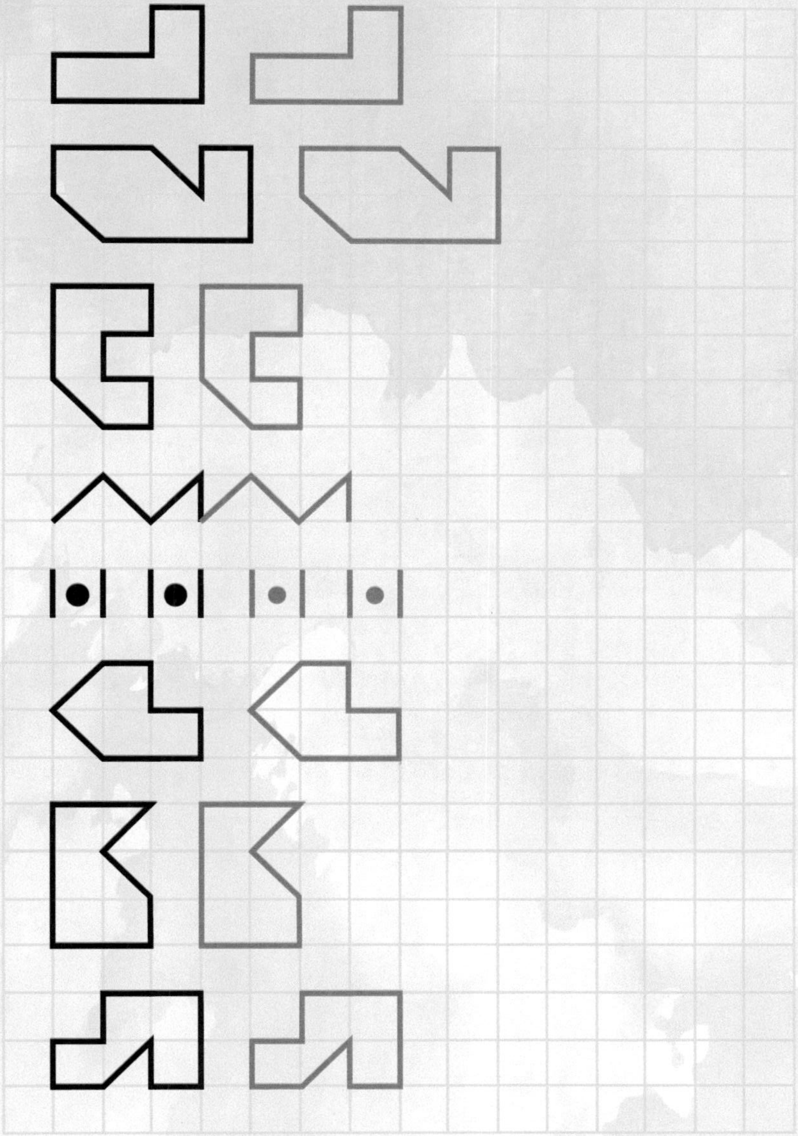

## 5. Money Handling:

***Materials Needed:*** **Play money, price tags, items to sell (like toys or household objects).**

### Steps:

i. Set up a small shop with priced items.

ii. Give the child a set amount of play money.

iii. Play roles where one is the buyer and the other the shopkeeper, using the money to conduct transactions.

# Fun Money Bank Notes

## 6. Time Telling Activities:

***Materials Needed:*** **Teaching clock with movable hands.**

### Steps:

i. **Start by showing the child the hour hand and how it relates to the numbers on the clock.**
ii. **Explain the minute hand and how it moves around the clock.**
iii. **Practice setting the clock to specific times and discussing what each time means in a daily context (like lunchtime or bedtime).**

the clock to specific times

Made in the USA
Columbia, SC
09 August 2024

40208686R00020